HOME SERIES

HOME SERIES
URBAN SPACES

BETA-PLUS

CONTENTS

P. 4-5 and p 10-11
A realization by the interior
architect Olivier Lempereur in
an apartment in Paris.

INTRODUCTION

F ar from the quietness of the countryside, many of us choose a city life. Living at the heart of activity, a home even more necessarily becomes a retreat and a defence against external aggression like noise or pollution. The interior consequently becomes synonymous with a decompression chamber and the hushed place where you can be protected from the tumult and recharge your batteries.

The residences shown in this work also display special attention to this protective place, in which the ambiance and decoration are primordial ingredients to create well-being in its occupants.

The city, yes, but not at any price. This volume presents top of the range and luxury interiors: spacious premises located in the centre of the city, a supreme luxury.

That's why followers of "never without my city" more often tend to these unusual spaces: disused factories or other buildings that have been converted into lofts. Visit these premises with a city-dweller's spirit for which the vocation is to offer a protective bubble.

Whether it relates to a sober loft in its own style, the intimate atmosphere of a manor house or an extravagant urban residence, each time the intent is to create a haven of unequalled peace, by which the construction or renovation are entirely determined by the lifestyle and personality of the occupants.

P. 8
Entrance hall to a
Parisian apartment
realized by Gérard
Faivre.
A prune coloured
carpet from
Toulemonde Bochard,
that strongly contrasts
with the orange of the
two chairs from
Modénature, its
complementary colour.

A LUMINOUS MINIMALISM

O livier Michel is a property developer and, as founder of Upptown, one of the project developers most talked of in recent months.

In a highly coveted district in the capital, he discovered a collection of abandoned warehouses and garages, which quickly transformed into a residential project comprising four ultramodern lofts.

The intention was initially to sell these four lofts, but Michel and his wife were so enthusiastic about the project that they decided to combine two of the units to create a massive unique plot, with a habitable surface area of over 600 m², supplemented by a garden, a swimming pool and two indoor patios.

The construction was entrusted to the architect Bruno Corbisier, the Upptown team took care of the interior design.

The floor surface is realised in epoxy, concrete was poured and then polished and covered with two top coats of paint. The black/white contrasts and the expressionist art by the Belgian painter Charles Szymkowicz make a dramatic effect.

Remember...

> A special place for artworks. A setting with value realised by the minimalist decoration of the premises: the immaculate white of the floors and the walls creates an ultra-contemporary effect.

> The black wall in the corridor. The strong and pigmented shades should often be preferred in passage areas to prevent fatigue to the eye while giving character to the space.

The swimming pool is surrounded by the loft and projects its blue reflections in every space.

Extremely glamorous harmony of silver and white: a wall padded with silver vinyl, a hearth from ABC interior covered in a sheet of stainless steel, the white epoxy floor and the sofa.

The large sofa from Minotti and the coffee table custom-made in varnished MDF, combined with a glossy black element.

Centred above the two stories, a
Lamorak d'Ipe Cavalli chandelier.
Sliding windows were provided
throughout this loft.

P. 18-21
Halogen spotlights from Modular. The support pillars
are surrounded with Jaga radiator elements.

The swimming pool is outdoors but highly integrated in the inside thanks to huge glazed picture windows without any joints.

The shower cubicle covered in black mosaic tiles is concealed behind a glazed wall of black enamel.

The wall seat covered in white leather offers a generous storage space. Drawings by Szymkowicz are displayed above.

P. 25-27
With the exception of the painting by
Charles Szymkowicz, the master
bedroom is virginal white. The Limited
Edition carpet gives it an intimate
character.
A bed by Ipe Cavalli is covered in
velvet. The bedside lights are from
Melograno.

Remember...

> Playing with materials and
the diversity of textures gives
all the sophistication to this
monochrome room.
Far from being cold, despite
the omnipresent white, the
room exudes warm and cosy
comfort.

A LOFT ON TWO FLOORS

T his loft on two floors is located in an old studio with rear house in the heart of Brussels.

The space was entirely redesigned by the architecture firm Olivier Dwek in cooperation with the architect Mathieu DeWitte.

The creation of a single volume on two floors allows a great incidence of light and optimal opening up of the space.

The library is presented as a living and functional object, with its monumental proportions and its different levels of depth.

It includes two levels of built-in stairs. The office of the owner of the premises is located on the top floor.

The library with its monumental dimensions is a creation by the firm Dwek. In the centre, in the foreground, an Indonesian pirogue nose. To the right a Scandia chair by the Norwegian designer Hans Brattrud. *Black & White Silver Gelatine Prints*, by Français Thierry Le Gouès.

To the left, an African millstone.
In the centre, in the rear a "Petit Jean",
by the Belgian sculptor James Lerooy.

Décor ideas

> Bring the sofa away from
the wall for a less
conventional layout. Here, the
symmetry around the low
table takes priority for a cosy
effect, despite the large
space.

> Break strict lines of the
furniture and the architecture
with another radically
different element: here a
low oval table to give a little
gentleness to this rather
masculine world.

P. 34-37
Groundpiece sofa from Flexform (at InStore).
Joinery in hand-brushed wenge and designed by the
architecture firm Olivier Dwek (a YKO realisation).
The sculpture on the pedestal is a sculpture package
by Kendell Geers (Rodolphe Janssen gallery). Table
Ado Chale in pepper grain.

The creation of a volume on two levels
gives luminosity and opens up the
space.

P. 38-39
Chairs by the great Danish designer Poul Kjaerholm (PK 9), produced by Kold
Christensen and found at the antiquarian Jerome Sohier.
A kitchen with an industrial spirit in brushed stainless steel.
In the rear, a canvas by the German painter Jonathan Meese.

Remember ...

> The return of the bed head is a strong trend. It makes it possible to dress the room and instantly gives it character.

WARMTH AND SOPHISTICATION

The new shop of Gilles de Meulemeester and his study agency Ebony in Paris consist of a sample of the style the interior architect represented over more than ten years and that he continues constantly to develop to create a timeless language of forms, simultaneously both classical and contemporary, which exude warmth and sophistication in an urban context.

P. 42-45
A work of art by Joëlle Callebaut overhangs an Atlanta sofa custom made by Ebony.
The coffee table in weathered Zebrano comes from Interni, as well as the light to the right of the sofa.
The carpet is made from silk and wool. The furniture surrounding the fireplace was made to measure by Ebony in smoked oak and provided with an Ecosmart system (which does not require any smoke discharge).

Remember...

> The sober, yet warm
shades – from beige to
chocolate – to create a
decoration without any
false notes, both elegant
and relaxing.

Dining table from Lessness and Seaton chairs. In the rear, a work of art by Ela Tom. To the right a lion by Jean-Philippe Serrano.

The pin oak Broadway table is combined with chairs of the Brussels model. The standing lamp In Between is also available from Ebony. Above the table, a work of art by a Belgian artist who answers to the pseudonym Dena.

Atlantis armchair with a Houston occasional table. The mirror was custom designed by Ebony. The triptych is by Florimond Dufoor. Ebony lamp.

The large sofa, Los Angeles model, was custom made. The coffee table and the occasional table are made from ebony. Milleraies carpet. The work of art is signed Jean-Luc Moerman.

The library furniture with office is
a creation by Ebony, realised in
smoked oak.

Remember...

> Rather than using a
decorative element above
the sofa, choose to dress
an empty wall with a large
canvas, to create a visual
balance.

RESTORATION OF AN ART NOUVEAU

MANOR HOUSE

The architect Jean-Baptiste Dewin was one of the figureheads of the second generation of art nouveau in the architecture line of the Vienna School, but always loyal to the principles of the art nouveau movement.

Work that is characterised by great formal soberness, precise geometry. This house from 1919 by Dewin is a very good example of this late art nouveau style.

It was restored in a contemporary fashion with respect for the authenticity of the building. The interior architecture was taken on by Hilde Cornelissen and by Ebony.

The office and the rooms around it were designed by Hilde Cornelissen. The two easy chairs are from Donghia. The original parquet was restored. The round table and the four chairs are a creation by Christian Liaigre.

The hall was repainted, restored to rediscover its original lustre.

P. 56 and above
The living room and dining room were designed by Hilde Cornelissen.
Above the Maxalto sofa, a canvas by Piet Bekaert.

Remember...

> The pattern of the parquet with a carpet effect is both discrete and decorative.

> The contrast between the poetic and white chandelier and the rigidity of the low table.

The Murano glass Donghia chandelier comes from Ebony.

The original granite floor
with mosaic pattern.

P. 63-65
The oak easy chairs with Africa leather are a creation by Promemoria.
Low Gandhi table from steel and bamboo from the Interni collection (all from Ebony). The two large Donghia sofas and the shelves were selected by Hilde Cornelissen.

A steel and wenge Housont occasional table from the Interni collection. The Donghia lamp is made from Murano glass and silk. These two objects were found at Ebony.

P. 66-67
The bedroom is a creation by Hilde Cornelissen.

The large lampshade from Ebony in pleated linen lights the dressing table of the master bedroom.

The bathroom is in Spanish Emperador marble.

Remember ...

> The wall cupboards located on either side of the corridor to the bathroom, an efficient and discrete storage solution.

CONTEMPORARY TRANSFORMATION

OF A CLASSICAL MANOR HOUSE

A young couple, passionate about architecture, transformed a manor house from 1910, in close cooperation with the interior architect Gilles de Meulemeester.

The main requirements requested by the owner, and realised masterfully by Gilles de Meulemeester, consisted of opening up the reception spaces to the maximum, allowing the light to enter and to give the house a more contemporary, intimate and pure feeling while preserving its charm and its original materials.

The top quality materials are used throughout this manor house and the sober colours dear to Gilles de Meulemeester can be found here. In the dining room, at the basement level, antique furniture has been combined with chairs from Promemoria.

The authentic tiles were kept in the kitchen.

Décor ideas

> Blend styles to create an original
kitchen: the mix of tiles paired with rustic
and modern furniture created this
undeniably charming décor.

The staircase hall was restored, the lift was masked with a glazed door with a decorative pattern.

Parquet of greyed oak.

Décor ideas

> A simple white picture rail animates the staircase wall.

> Give preference to colour on the walls rather than on the wood for a less classical atmosphere.

The office is a creation by Ebony, as well as the suspension. Chair from Promemoria.

P. 76-77
The dressing area was entirely realised in grey oak.

View of the dressing room
from the bedroom.

Décor idea

> The ingenious oak partition
works as a bed head while
concealing a practical storage
area.

The parents' bathroom is realised in Azul Cascais natural stone.
Taps from Tara de Dornbracht. Original photographs by Caroline Notté.

The partition in the children's bathroom
is partly covered in metro tiles. The
floor tiles are by Agnès Emery.

PURE BEAUTY

T he interior architect François Marcq has transformed a large space into a personal pied-à-terre: an unusual project, of a pure and natural beauty.

The characteristics of the loft were respected: waxed concrete floor, rough materials like the concrete ceiling and the iron picture windows.

The creation of perspectives is of primordial importance in François Marcq's approach: he hates closed rooms.

Remember...

> Carpets warm the floor and create distinct areas of rest. Without them, the armchairs appear lost and their layout inconsistent.

François Marcq adores natural materials, durable materials and those that age well.

Décor ideas

> An original but successful layout: the mirror over the wash basin is located in front of the window. A layout that emphasises the graphic nature of the elements.

> The large wall mirror makes it possible almost to double the feeling of space while accentuating the luminosity.

SUBTLE BALANCE

L ocated in natural surroundings but close to the city centre: this exceptional home offers the best of both worlds.

Originally, the home was built just before the Second World War. It was transformed profoundly the first time by architect Philippe Cuylits in the 1980's.

Fifteen years later, its residents involved Joël Claisse, who only kept the stairs, the dining room, the living room and hearth at the end of major works. The volumes and the living areas were visibly extended; the impression felt is that of light, space and perfectly balanced lines that appear both timeless and contemporary: a genuinely pleasant house that reflects calm and serenity.

A double living space was added to the main cuboid building.

The residents are true art enthusiasts: works by Sugimoto, Gormley, Horn…

The stairs, varnished in mid-grey, is one of the only remaining elements of the old residence.

The dining room, more informal, includes furniture by Philippe Hurel.

Remember...

> Lights placed directly on the drilled table to allow the wires to pass through it.
An original solution to dinner lighting.

The kitchen, in shades of sand
and Bordeaux, was realised by
Obumex in partnership with
the architect Joël Claisse.

P. 102-105
The general use of earthen colours and natural
materials creates an intimate and serene atmosphere,
reflecting subtle balance.

Remember...

> The columns with integrated lighting frame the wash basin unit.

> The tiling is replaced by different species of wood to create a cosy bathroom.

THE RETREAT

OF AN ART COLLECTOR

C laire Bataille and Paul Ibens have designed an apartment for a passionate collector of modern art.

The contribution of the principal was very important to this project: numerous pieces from the collection give a highly personal touch to the realisation.

The oak floor was blanched and the walls painted white. Fabrics in pearl grey silk by Jab.
Room dividers were installed in this space evocative of a loft, to exhibit the works of art.

Décor ideas

> Select numerous sofa ends and bring them to create an unconventional coffee table.

To the left on the photo, two easy chairs by Christian Liaigre. The hearth was realised entirely in Pietra Serena.
To the left of the hearth, an iron cupboard. To the right, an armchair by Axel Vervoordt covered in white fabric.

In the background, a large canvas by Paladino. The table is a personal design in rough oak.

The owner's major collection of artwork was completed by a large number of her finds.
The cupboard with glass shelves is a project by Bataille-ibens; an antique belonging to the occupant is on the top.

Remember…

> The maxi lampshade overturns the rather classical ambiance.

> The desk and the folding chair give lightness to this room furnished with rather massive elements.

MAKE OVER OF

A DISUSED SHELL

A disused shell captured the attention of a passionate lover of architecture. He envisaged creating his residence in collaboration with the architect Bruno Erpicum. A few quality elements were retained to form the volume created in the property.

A brick wall was discovered. It runs alongside the road to become the interior façade of the hall and kitchen, it continues outside and encloses the garden. The residence benefits for the entire height of the property; the office is arranged higher up, between the metal beams.

More contained, the bedrooms are located in a massive volume, a container. They each benefit from an opening onto the garden to the side, the water rooms are provided with light from two interior picture windows. The rough materials are put in the limelight, the new elements are plastered or concreted, the polished concrete floor slabs reflect the light.

The kitchen is installed in perspective, it opens onto the garden.

The original structure – metal joinery
and pillars – is preserved.
The furniture was chosen by Dominique
Rigo.

Remember...

> A monastic room in which the decorative force emanates from a deliberate minimalism coupled with highly present architectural elements like the brick column that is thereby emphasised.

> The floor carpet positioned in a decentralised way again emphasises the graphic nature of the whole.

HOME SERIES

Volume 11 : URBAN SPACES

The reports in this book are selected from the Beta-Plus collection of home-design books: www.betaplus.com
They have been compiled in a special series by Le Figaro in French language: Ma Déco

PUBLISHER

Beta-Plus Publishing
Termuninck 3
B – 7850 Enghien
Belgium
www.betaplus.com
info@betaplus.com

TEXT
Alexandra Druesne

PHOTOGRAPHY
Jo Pauwels

DESIGN
Polydem - Nathalie Binart

TRANSLATIONS
Txt-Ibis

ISBN : 978-90-8944-042-6

Printed in China

P. 126-127
A design by Bruno Erpicum.